Genre **Biography**

? Essential Question
What can people do to b.....y about
a positive change?

Jane Addams
A Woman of Action
by Jane Buxton

PEACE

Chapter 1

Early Years

What do you want to do with your life? Jane Addams thought about this a lot when she was a child.

Jane was born in 1860, and she grew up in Cedarville, Illinois. Her mother died when Jane was two and a half years old. Jane's father took care of her and her sisters. Mr. Addams was a rich man. He was also a **philanthropist**, a person who helps others.

As a young girl, Jane wanted to make a difference in the world.

2

Jane loved her father and wanted to be like him. He taught her to be kind and **tolerant**, or respectful of other people's opinions. He also taught her to love learning and reading.

Jane cared about people. At a young age, she saw that some people were rich and others were poor. Some people lived in nice, big homes in one neighborhood. Other people lived in small houses in another place.

Jane's father was a landowner, miller, and banker.

People had **unequal** lives. Jane dreamed of living in a big house with small houses nearby.

Jane wanted to be a doctor so she could help the poor. But her father wanted her to have a family. Jane did not want to get married, but she did not want to **defy** her father.

Addams studied at a women's college called Rockford Female Seminary. She was good at reading, writing, and public speaking.

Addams (back row) made some good friends at school.

When Addams was 21 years old, her father died. Addams was **devastated** and shocked. She went to school to become a doctor, but she was too sad to study. She had other problems. A curve in her spine made it painful to sit for many hours. Then she became very ill. As a result, she gave up her dream of becoming a doctor.

Addams went overseas after she left college. In London, she saw many people living in terrible **poverty**. She wanted to help, but she did not know how. She returned home.

A few years later, Jane went back to London. She visited a place called Toynbee Hall in a poor part of London. Toynbee Hall was an experiment. A group of educated young men wanted to make the lives of poor people better. Toynbee Hall was known as a settlement house because the men who worked there also settled there to live. They offered classes in singing, reading, and drawing.

Now Addams knew what she wanted to do. She would set up a settlement house back home! She was very excited.

STOP AND CHECK

Who taught Jane Addams to help other people?

Extreme Poverty

Once Addams visited a London market. The market was closing. Rotten food was being sold at a cheap price. Addams saw thin people dressed in rags trying to buy it. These people were *very* poor and hungry. Addams never forgot them.

Addams Takes Action

Back in Illinois, Addams and her friend, Ellen Starr, looked for a house to rent. They found an enormous, old house in a poor neighborhood in Chicago. The house was called Hull House, and the friends would model it after Toynbee Hall.

Most wealthy, or rich, Americans didn't know how bad things were for the poor. Addams and Starr decided that Hull House would have two purposes. One purpose was to give wealthy people the chance to learn about poor people by helping them.

STOP AND CHECK

How was Hull House like Addams's dream?

Hull House was first owned by a businessman named Charles Hull.

Bettmann/CORBIS

The other purpose was to make the lives of working people better. They would give them **opportunities** that were usually **reserved**, or saved, for the rich, such as education and music lessons.

Addams and Starr wanted educated women and men to live at Hull House. They wanted them to get to know their neighbors, who were neither rich nor educated. They would set up clubs, classes, and events for the local people.

Addams used her own money to fix up Hull House. She also **sought** money from other wealthy citizens. This money would help keep the house running.

Life in the City

When Addams and Starr set up Hull House, many people were coming to America from Europe. They were looking for a better life.

Many moved to Chicago to find work. Women, men, and even children worked long days and nights. They worked in unsafe places and were not paid much. Business owners became very rich.

With great **anticipation**, Addams and Starr opened Hull House in 1889. Many people wanted to help her. They moved into Hull House, too.

Hull House was a popular place for local people to meet. They could take classes there, too. Soon, Hull House had a kitchen, a gymnasium, and a music school for people to use. There was even a theater, a library, and an art gallery. Hull House also helped people who needed childcare, or help from a doctor or lawyer.

Many people visited Hull House. They liked what they saw happening there.

Addams started clubs for children.

Valuing Traditions

Addams set up a museum at Hull House to teach the visitors about the older immigrants in the neighborhood. The older immigrants were able to share their knowledge of traditional arts and crafts with visitors. Addams wanted to show that the skills of these older people were still important.

Addams was a kind person. She was an **outspoken advocate** for the poor, and she inspired many people to help others. She became famous because of her work. Settlement houses were set up in other cities.

Addams wrote 13 books.

But Hull House needed money to keep going. Addams began to write books. She was a good writer, and her autobiography, *Twenty Years at Hull House,* became famous. She sold many books. The money she made from writing was used to support her work.

STOP AND CHECK

What kinds of things could people do at Hull House?

Chapter 3

Changing the World

During Addams's life, many women, men, and children from poor areas of Chicago went to work. Most of them worked in factories. The conditions were terrible. They worked long hours and were not paid very much. However, if they didn't work, they would starve.

Addams heard a terrible story. Three children were hurt at a factory. One of them died. The machine they used was dangerous. Addams asked the factory owner to make the machine safe. The owner **refused** and wouldn't change it. Addams was shocked.

Children often worked in factories like this one.

Children Are Cheap

Most factory owners did not want child labor laws to change. They said that hard work taught children good values. They said that families needed the money the children earned. Child labor made it cheaper to run their businesses. They didn't have to pay children as much as adults. Child labor was finally banned in 1938.

Addams knew that she could not help the poor by herself. She also knew that poverty would not stop unless the laws were changed.

So she talked to politicians about changing the laws. Addams wanted to make things better for workers. She wanted people to work in safe conditions. She wanted to limit how many hours people worked in a day. And she worked hard to make school free for all children.

Things didn't change right away, but people listened to Addams. Others spoke out, too, and people started to think differently. Slowly the laws were **reformed**.

Addams knew that changing the world was hard. She needed to change people's attitudes first. Addams is known for her work helping others, but she also worked to help groups of people. Some people were treated unfairly because of their race. So Addams helped start the American Civil Liberties Union (ACLU) and the National Association for the Advancement of Colored People (NAACP). Both of these organizations are still around today.

Everyone Is Responsible

Jane Addams believed that everyone has a responsibility to help others. She worked to help women, children, and ethnic minorities. She also worked for better health care for the poor, and for peace. Addams asked, what is more important than having "faith in new possibilities and the courage to advocate them?"

Addams also tried to change people's minds about war. She thought that war was wrong. She even tried to stop World War I.

Addams talked to people about peace. She helped start some groups for women, including the Women's Peace Party, the International Congress of Women, and the Women's International League for Peace and Freedom.

Members of the Women's Peace Party in 1915.

Not everyone agreed with Addams. Some people wrote her nasty letters. Newspapers that didn't agree with her work **criticized** and spoke against her. However, Addams knew she was **entitled** to speak out. Addams kept working for change and for peace.

Jane Addams is one of America's best-loved women leaders. Addams was **courageous**, or brave. She was often sick, but that did not stop her. She never gave up her goal of helping others.

In 1931, Addams received the Nobel Peace Prize. The award was in **recognition** of her work.

STOP AND CHECK

Which groups of people did Addams try to help?

Addams was the first American woman to receive the Nobel Peace Prize.

Time Line: Jane Addams	
1860	born, Cedarville, IL
1881	graduates from Rockford Female Seminary
1887	visits Toynbee Hall
1889	sets up Hull House
1909	helps set up NAACP
1910	publishes *Twenty Years at Hull House*
1915	helps set up the Women's Peace Party and organizes the International Congress of Women
1919	helps set up the Women's International League for Peace and Freedom
1920	helps set up the American Civil Liberties Union
1931	receives the Nobel Peace Prize
1935	dies, Chicago, IL

Bettmann/CORBIS

Respond to Reading

Summarize

Use important details from *Jane Addams: A Woman of Action* to summarize the life of Jane Addams. Your graphic organizer may help you.

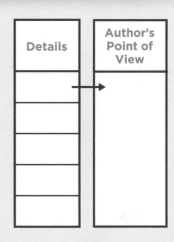

Details | Author's Point of View

Text Evidence

1. What does the author think about Addams? How can you tell? AUTHOR'S POINT OF VIEW

2. Turn to page 6. What does the word *wealthy* mean? How do you know? VOCABULARY

3. Reread pages 10–11. Jane Addams worked to stop child labor. Write about what the author thinks about this. Use details from the text in your answer. WRITE ABOUT READING

Compare Texts
Read about a positive change
for Mexican Americans.

Gus García
Takes on Texas

In 1950, a man in Jackson County, Texas, was arrested. His name was Pete Hernández. His mother asked a lawyer, Gustavo C. García, to help her son.

García was a Mexican American. He believed that people of all races deserved a fair trial.

The law said that anyone could be on a jury. However, Mexican Americans, African Americans, and women were never chosen for juries. García thought that a jury that was too different from a **defendant** could not be **neutral**.

Gustavo C. García was a lawyer in Texas.

García said he would help Hernández. He thought this case could be a way to change the **judicial system**. He asked other lawyers for help.

There were no Mexican Americans on the jury in Hernández's trial. García told the judge this was unfair. The judge didn't agree. He said it was only by accident that there were no Hispanic people on the jury. The lawyers were ready for the judge's answer. They showed him court records. The records showed that no one with a Hispanic name had ever been on a jury in Jackson County.

The judge still disagreed. Hernández was given a life sentence. García appealed to another court, which turned him down.

García decided to appeal to the United States Supreme Court. This would be risky and expensive. However, if the lawyers won, it would mean a positive change for Mexican Americans.

Many people knew about the case. Poor Hispanic people raised money to help García fight for them.

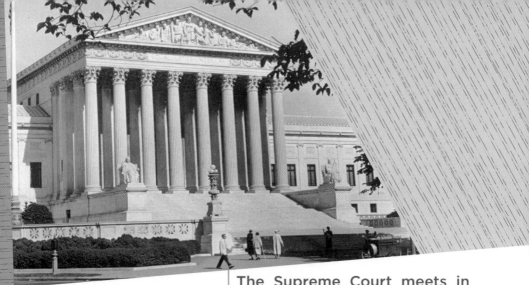

The Supreme Court meets in this building in Washington D.C.

The Supreme Court listened to García. It was the first time the Supreme Court had made a decision about the rights of Mexican Americans. The court said Hernández should get another trial. This time, Mexican Americans would be on the jury. The jury would also include other groups that had not been on juries before.

García and his team had made history. Now everyone could be part of the jury system.

Endnote: At his second trial, Pete Hernández was found guilty again.

Make Connections

Why did García want to change the jury system in Texas? ESSENTIAL QUESTION

What kind of people were Jane Addams and Gustavo C. García? TEXT TO TEXT

Glossary

advocate *(AD-vuh-kuht)* someone who supports or promotes the interests of someone else *(page 9)*

defendant *(di-FEN-duhnt)* the person who is being accused in court *(page 16)*

judicial system *(jew-DI-shuhl SIS-tuhm)* the courts and the branch of government that enforces laws *(page 17)*

philanthropist *(fuh-LAN-thruh-pist)* a person who cares about humankind and does kind and charitable deeds *(page 2)*

poverty *(PAH-vuhr-tee)* the state of being very poor *(page 5)*

reformed *(ri-FORMD)* changed for the better *(page 11)*

Index

Focus on
Social Studies

Purpose To understand how changes in the past have made a difference to our lives today

What to Do

Step 1 ▶ Imagine it is 100 years ago. You work in a factory. What is your life like? Talk about this with a small group. Use information from the text to help you.

Step 2 ▶ Draw a chart with two columns. Label one column "100 Years Ago." List the things you have to do each day. Don't forget, your day might begin before sunrise.

Step 3 ▶ Label the other column "Today." List the things you usually do each day. Include the things you learn at school and the things you do after school, too.

Step 4 ▶ Talk about the two lists with your group. What things are the same? What things are different?